D1232283

Living on the Edge:
Spiritual Help for the Soul
Under Attack

Michael S. Pitts

Cornerstone Publications
Toledo, Ohio

Unless otherwise indicated, all scriptural quotations are from the
King James Version of the Bible.

Living on the Edge: Spiritual Help for the Soul Under Attack
Published by:
Cornerstone Publications
P.O. Box 351690
Toledo, OH 43635
ISBN 0-9633583-2-4

Second Printing, May 1997

Copyright © 1994 by Cornerstone Publications
All rights reserved.
Reproduction of text in whole or in part without the express written con-
sent by the author is not permitted and is unlawful according to the 1976
United States Copyright Act.

Editorial Consultant: Phyllis Mackall, Broken Arrow, OK

Cover design and book production by:
DB & Associates Design Group, Inc.
P.O. Box 52756, Tulsa, OK 74152
Cover illustration is protected by the 1976 United States Copyright Act.
Copyright © 1994 by DB & Associates Design Group, Inc.

Printed in the United States of America.

Contents

Chapter 1
Modern Life: Stressed Out!

Early in 1993, Hollywood released a film starring Michael Douglas that was entitled "Falling Down." It was a story about a day in the life of a man who had experienced all he could take of the pressures, disappointments, and inconveniences of life.

In the movie, the main character experiences mounting anxiety as he endures a traffic jam (caused by construction), suffers the oppression of inflated prices at a local store (owned by a "foreigner"), and is put through the indignities of poor service (with a smile) at a fast-food restaurant.

These everyday frustrations, combined with a sense of being disconnected from his family (the result of recent divorce), and the loss of his job, culminate on this fateful day to push him over the edge!

As a result of all these pressures, his normal, healthy logic and rationale are suspended, and he resorts to violence, murder, and the using of explosives!

Sound bizarre? It wasn't too long ago that our nation was baffled by the explanation of a San Francisco city employee who had just shot the mayor and a city supervisor. He claimed he was not responsible for his actions because he had just eaten a "Twinkie"!

We are all too familiar today with the stories of psychopaths like Jeffrey Dahmer, the serial killer who not only brutalized and killed his victims, but also cut them up and ate them!

Add to that reports of people like David Koresh, the Waco, Texas, religious zealot who is neither the first nor the last to claim to be the Son of God. He joins a long list of others, including Charles Manson, Jim Jones, and a long-haired street person a few miles from my home.

The Frustration Level Rises

Amid these widely publicized, bizarre cases, anger and frustration seem to be on the rise among the general population. Television talk host Oprah Winfrey recently aired a program where people explained why they felt like they were about to "lose it."

During her hour-long show, people expressed their feelings of helplessness. One mother was upset with teachers who, in her opinion, were not teaching their students and, furthermore, exhibited a "careless" attitude.

Her intense emotions were matched by a disheartened teacher who felt overwhelmed by overcrowded classrooms, low salaries, the ever-growing threat of violence, and the exorbitant amount of time spent in dealing with undisciplined children who have no structure at home and resist it at school.

Other guests expressed anger on topics ranging from insurance companies, the health care system, and the way drivers behave at a four-way stop intersection!

Perils of Air Travel

If I haven't made the point that people seem to be stressed out, it might be important to tell you that I am writing the first draft of this book as I sit delayed at O'Hare Airport in Chicago. The airline asked everyone to exit the plane just as a businessman said out loud, "It feels good to be on time for a change!"

I probably should also mention that a few minutes prior to this delay, I found myself surrounded by several Chicago police officers who were apprehending a young woman who claimed she had put a bomb aboard one of the aircraft!

We certainly live in an increasingly oppressive environment; and each of us, whether we know it or not, is in contact daily with people who are on the edge — people who are struggling to survive — people who are losing the battle.

The purpose of this book is not to make one paranoid (no pun intended). After all, most of us seem to be navigating the treacherous waters of life without running aground too often.

Why We Act the Way We Do

It is our aim, however, to provide help and healing to those in need as well as answers to those who have wondered why we do the things we do. What *motivates* us? What *limits* us? What *defines* us?

With knowledge comes the power to change; the power to break negative cycles that may have been in your family for years; the power to live above self-defeating habits; the power to live a life above the damaging effects of stress and anxiety. And above all, with knowledge comes the power to love your neighbor and yourself.

The Greatest Commandment

When asked by a Pharisee what the greatest commandment was, Jesus answered:

Thou shalt love the Lord thy God with all thy heart, and with all thy soul, and with all thy mind.

This is the first and great commandment.

And the second is like unto it, Thou shalt love thy neighbor as thyself.

Matthew 22:37-39

We must correctly *define* ourselves before we can correctly *align* ourselves. Therefore, let us endeavor to define what is the "self" of man. We will begin by taking a closer look at the revolutionary statement Jesus made in Matthew 22.

"Thou shalt love the Lord thy God with all thy heart...."

The *heart* is the seat of your emotions. God wants you to involve emotion in your relationship with Him. Worship is not facts and theories, and salvation must do more than teach you God's policies. It must cause you to relate to Him as a Person.

"With all thy soul...."

The *soul* is the seat of your personality — that which defines you and sets you apart from all others. There is no one else in the world just like you!

God *delights* in the splendid diversity of His people. He *enjoys* the uniqueness you bring to Him. He *likes* it when you break out of cookie-cutter Christianity and refuse to be a face in the crowd, choosing instead to display that you are a child of the King. As we will see later, the soul is the "self" of man.

"...and with all thy mind."

The *mind* is the seat of your intellect. The more you know about God, the greater is your capacity for worship. Although His thoughts are higher than ours, our efforts to know Him offer us an inexhaustible adventure. He opens His eternal being to us and says, "Spend your life searching for the depths of Me with all your mind; with all you have. You will never reach the end of learning about Me."

Man lives in, and has contact with, three distinct spheres of influence. Therefore, God has made man a triune being. That is to say, *man is one whole made up of three parts: body, spirit, and soul.* Let's look closer at the creation of man:

The Body

"And the Lord God formed man of the dust of the ground..." (Genesis 2:7).

This refers to man's body. *With our body we contact the material world.* The physical senses of the body include sight, smell, taste, touch, and hearing.

The body is both visible and temporary. Because it is made of the earth, the body cannot enter into another non-tangible dimension. After death, of course, the body returns to the earth — to the dust from which it came.

The Spirit

"...and breathed into his nostrils the breath of life..."

This refers to spirit *(pneuma* — breath). *With our spirit we contact the spirit world.* We can know or discern with our spirit (Romans 8). Our spirit is born again at conversion (John 3). We worship God in our spirit (John 4).

The spirit of man is *invisible* and *eternal.* The spirit of man has expression and contact with the material world through the use of a body.

The Soul

"...and man became a living soul."

This refers to *psyche* or "self." *With our soul we contact the psychological world.*

Our *personality* is contained within our soul. We emote and interact on an intimate, personal level through our soul. The soul is where we carry our memories, feelings, belief systems, and emotional prints of life. As we saw, the soul is the "self" *(psyche);* and psychology is the study of self. The soul is also the source of *the will.*

Because God is the Creator of the "self," it is only through Him that modern men and women can ever hope to achieve victorious living. *Having a proper, healthy self-image comes from seeing oneself in the light of God's Word and His plan for man.*

A Living Soul

Man did not become just *a* soul; he became a *living* soul. That is to say, God created man as the sole master of his own eternal destiny. A "living" soul means man has the ability to make decisions and determine his ultimate future. Therefore, man is what we commonly call "a free moral agent."

If you *decide* to serve *God* and make appropriate actions to do so, friends, family, adversity, and the devil himself are all powerless to stop you.

If you *decide* to serve *the devil* and make appropriate actions to do so, friends, family, adversity, and God Himself are all powerless to stop you.

Other forces — some that help and some that hinder — may influence your choice, but *you alone choose your eternal destiny.* As God says in His Word: "...I have set before *you* life and death, blessing and cursing: therefore *choose* life..." (Deuteronomy 30:19) and "...*choose* you this day whom ye will serve..." (Joshua 24:15).

Man's Powerful Will

The will of man is powerful. In fighting disease, the will to live is an important part of regaining health. In breaking addictions and habits, the will is the single most important factor. It provides what we call will-power!

When the will is strong and is properly exercised, it brings the body (*sarx*, the source of the sin nature) and the soul (*psyche*, emotions or self) under the leadership of the Holy Spirit.

Second Timothy 1:7 (*Twentieth Century New Testament*) says, "The Spirit which God gave us was not to inspire us with cowardice, but with power, love, and self-control." *The King James Version* translates the last phrase as "sound mind."

Chapter 2

Emotional Wholeness

Beloved, I wish above all things that thou mayest prosper and be in health, even as thy soul prospereth.

3 John 2

As a result of demonic attacks on the soul, man seeks in vain to have his drives, desires, and emotional needs met, making him a slave — and producing an obsessive, compulsive, addictive society.

In modern society, we are plagued, as never before, by the following manifestations of souls who are losing the battle against demonic forces.

1. *Chemical addictions:* Crack cocaine, nerve pills, caffeine, alcohol, sleeping pills, cigarettes

2. *Eating disorders:* Bulimia, anorexia, gluttony

3. *Emotional disorders:* Anti-social, extramarital affairs, co-dependency, infatuation, stalking

4. *Psychosexual dysfunctions:* Homosexuality, lesbianism, transvestite, incest, pornography, voyeurism, transsexual

5. *Mental illness:* Personality disorders, phobias, increasing insanity, depression, hysteria

Nervous breakdowns, panic attacks, depression, paranoia, hysteria, and so forth are the manifestations of a soul that is losing the battle against demonic forces.

Mental Health Defined

In their book *Introduction to Psychology and Counseling*, Paul D. Meier, M.D., Frank B. Minirth, M.D., and Frank B. Wichern, Ph.D., have stated that people are considered to be mentally healthy if they are: (1) In contact with reality, and (2) sufficiently free of anxiety so they are not significantly incapacitated functionally, socially, or biologically for any extended period of time.

The doctors go on to list a dozen or so characteristics of mentally healthy people, 10 of which I have adopted and amplified for this book.

1. A healthy person exhibits the ability to function at full capacity both intellectually and emotionally.

The inability to keep a train of thought or incoherent sentence structure could be signs of trouble; especially if these symptoms are accompanied by unwarranted crying or anger.

2. A healthy person demonstrates that he or she is in contact with reality by reacting to life's situations in a realistic manner.

Therefore, a person with a healthy soul does not punch holes in the wall during domestic disputes. Neither does he beat his car with a sledgehammer when it breaks down!

3. A healthy person approaches life with self-confidence, optimism, and a sense of humor.

When people are tormented by the forces of demonic oppression, they develop a pessimistic view of life. Even if the victims do not understand the presence of these forces, their effects are felt. The victims lose the wonderful human ability to roll with life's punches by finding humor in their situation. They may even become hostile toward others who try to make them laugh or see the good in spite of the bad. In short, they take everything too seriously!

4. A healthy person has an unwavering purpose for life.

Those who have received wholeness from Christ know that every day can be an adventure in faith. They know that even when things seem to be going wrong, they will keep on living, their confidence being firmly based in God's goodness.

On the other hand, a person who is losing the battle of daily life sometimes gives in to the damaging thoughts of "ending it all" when life seems unbearable. In other words, he develops a suicidal tendency.

I have seen this spirit attack teenagers who should have everything to live for, but because a boyfriend or a girlfriend broke up with them, they thought there was no reason to live.

The suicidal tendency is a strong force that is growing in our generation. Its effects are felt everywhere from Wall Street to college campuses. But the Bible tells us that Jesus came that we might have abundant *life* (John 10:10)!

5. A healthy person relates well to a variety of people with the capacity for intimacy.

Antisocial and reclusive behavior is a danger sign. Healthy people enjoy being around other people. People who are in bondage often retreat from society and drop out of life. Often they surround themselves with a large number of animals, such as cats or dogs. They then become unkept and live like and relate more readily to these animals.

Prejudice also falls into this category of bondage. A healthy person accepts the fact that others have different life experiences, national or racial origins, and economic conditions. The healthy person feels neither inferior or superior to people who are different from himself.

6. A healthy person accepts the authority of legitimate people and institutions.

Rebellion is not the product of a healthy soul. Those who are continually challenging the authority of their parents, teachers, pastors, employers, and law officials are people who often have deep-rooted emotional problems.

7. A healthy person lives a balanced life and knows how to care for himself and others.

A healthy person functions in both dependent and independent roles. This means striking a balance between the organizational and creative sides of one's personality.

A self-centered person must always have things his or her way. On the other hand, there are some people who spend all their energy helping others until they themselves suffer physically, emotionally, and financially.

8. A healthy person is dependable.

People who are in control of their lives have *"self-authority."* This means they are able to make a commitment and follow through on it.

All of us know people who are not taken seriously when they speak, because they have a track record of being undependable. When a person is consistently late for work, church, or other functions, it is usually a sign that his or her life is out of order. Remember, when a person never fulfills his obligations or keeps his word, there is an underlying cause.

9. A healthy person has the ability to express and control emotions.

A person walking in wholeness neither gravitates toward nor seeks to avoid strong emotional settings.

An emotionally stable person can be where God wants him to be and who God wants him to be. If the situation or the environment call for strong emotions — be it laughing, shouting, dancing, or crying — the emotionally strong individual is not nervous. He or she is equally comfortable when it is time to be still and quiet.

The one who without restraints continually expresses his feelings, and the one who always speaks his mind have something in common: They are both in bondage, just as is the one who never interacts!

10. Healthy persons are satisfied with their maleness or femaleness, as God has created them.

People who are healthy in their souls should enjoy a satisfactory sex life *within the bounds of marriage.*

But when people are demonically influenced, they can become confused about their sexuality. In such cases, a man thinks he is really *a woman* trapped in a man's body, or a woman thinks she is really *a man* trapped in a woman's body! Others begin to lust after members of their same sex. (God, however, is not confused.)

Out of Control?

When God created man as "a living soul," He gave him the gift of self-control. Man demonstrates this by his ability to choose corresponding actions and responses for his environment.

Yet, unfortunately, some have lost the self-control God gave them, and they are now *out of control.* Therefore, when they are placed in certain settings or situations, they find themselves powerless to make the proper responses or choices. Satan drives them by an unseen force, sets them up — and they fail over and over again.

Maybe it's the alcoholic who feels overpowered by his need to drink, the adulterer or fornicator whose lust is never satisfied, or the person whose temper explodes without warning into a rage.

How does this happen? How does a person lose control over his self or soul? We will answer this in the next chapter.

Chapter 3
Losing Control

I have come up with six primary ways in which a person may lose control over his self (or soul). I'm sure there are more.

1. Altered consciousness

God placed your mind at the seat of your consciousness to govern what enters your spirit. Much like the lid on a container, you "open" yourself up to some influences and "close" yourself off to others.

When your consciousness is *altered*, it is as if the lid has been removed, and thus you may become highly susceptible to evil spirits which seek to control humans.

Altered states of consciousness are caused by such things as:

(a) Drugs

When a person is drunk, he is said to have lower inhibitions. Many drugs distort a person's view of reality. Seeking to escape, he ends up enslaved.

(b) Hypnosis

It is both foolish and dangerous to give entry to your inner man to another person. Hypnosis bypasses the natural safeguard God gave you. Once the seal to the subconscious is broken, a person becomes more open to unconscious or spiritual forces.

During hypnosis, you are not in full control of your thoughts, and you may become easily influenced by the suggestions and the conditioning of another.

(c) Subliminal tapes/music

As with hypnosis, subliminal messages bypass the door to the "self," which is the conscious mind. They condition, reinforce, and program a message to produce a desired response. And often people get more than they bargained for!

The Bible's answer is:

...He that entereth not by the door into the sheepfold, but climbeth up some other way, the same is a thief and a robber.

John 10:1

Let this mind be in you, which was also in Christ Jesus.

Philippians 2:5

2. Continually yielding to wrong desires

If a person, in anger, continues to lack self-control and yields to violence, destruction of property, vocal outbursts, and other destructive impulses, he will eventually hand over control of his "self" to other forces; demonic forces.

Then he will find he is no longer in charge of his temper. The same will hold true of his thought life, sexual appetites, attitudes and so forth. Continual yielding leads to habits and habits create a lifestyle.

The Bible's answer is:

Neither yield ye your members as instruments of unrighteousness unto sin: but yield yourselves unto God....

Romans 6:13

...know ye not that your body is the temple of the Holy Ghost which is in you....

1 Corinthians 6:19

3. The way we process the actions of others

When people do not have the benefit of God's truth concerning the issues of life, they are forced to process the actions of others through their own limited experiences. Often this leads them to false conclusions and deception.

For example, some schools are teaching youngsters that men and women can be born as homosexuals. If the students accept this premise, which is not true, they will walk in deception and will be in bondage.

In the case of child abuse, the abuser is solely to blame. Yet many victims of child abuse believe *they* were somehow at fault. If the victims never know the truth concerning their innocence, they may develop self-damaging belief systems producing low self-esteem, self-destructive behavior, and even self-hatred.

The Bible's answer is:

And ye shall know the truth, and the truth shall make you free.

John 8:32

4. Proper development is interrupted

Humans develop, learn, and comprehend throughout different stages in their lives. Child care professionals tell us that 85 percent of a child's personality is developed before he or she is 5 years of age!

Children develop different cognitive skills early in life. At other ages or levels, they are ready to understand abstract thought and relational or self concepts.

For example, somewhere between the ages of 3 and 6, children begin to formulate their concept of sexual identity, which simply means they know they are either a boy or a girl. They are also able to divide other children into the categories of boys or girls.

Obviously, if children are sexually violated during this crucial time in their development, they can be damaged to the point where only Jesus can repair them. Thank God He can!

Puberty is another critical time of development. When young people are robbed of their childhood, their normal sexual development is perverted, and they loose the "building blocks" that are crucial for developing proper self-esteem. Furthermore, people may lose control over their self if proper development is interrupted.

The Bible's answer is:

Train up a child in the way he should go: and when he is old, he will not depart from it.

Proverbs 22:6

5. By wrong associations

As we are growing up, we have a tendency to believe that everyone's world is similar to ours. Therefore, we accept our experiences as "normal," even if they are not.

This is how abuse, poverty, addictions, and failure are handed down from one generation to another. A child does not know he is poor until someone tells him he is, or until he sees or experiences a better lifestyle.

Usually people become like those with whom they associate. If a boy is raised among fathers, uncles, cousins, and male friends who are all alcoholics or cheat on their wives, he will grow up thinking this behavior is normal. Likewise, girls who have watched their mothers being physically dominated often will permit men in their relationships to behave this way, thinking it is normal.

The Bible's answer is:

He that walketh with wise men shall be wise: but a companion of fools shall be destroyed.

Proverbs 13:20

6. Trauma

Last, the devil will take advantage of tragedy and use it as a tool to *depress, oppress,* and even *possess* people.

The traumatic death of a loved one can be used by the devil to allow a spirit of grief to enter an individual. We all know someone who has lost a loved one and has *"never been the same since."*

16

Another example is found in the lives of business people who lose a lot of money in a deal or on the stock market, and they kill themselves.

It is not uncommon for children who have been violently sexually abused to develop "split" or multiple personalities. If more than one personality is living in your body, all but the original one that God placed there need to be cast out!

During tragedy and adversity, the prosperous soul is supported by and is under the greater control of the Holy Spirit. This allows believers to maintain their balance and continue to live happy lives in spite of external circumstances.

The Bible's answer is:

When the enemy shall come in like a flood, the Spirit of the Lord shall lift up a standard against him.

Isaiah 59:19

The Quest for Self-Esteem

People do many things — even bizarre things — to make them feel better about themselves. They seek to accumulate wealth, submit to silicone implants, or dangerously starve their bodies in a frantic quest to be "fashionable."

For some, work and success become an all-consuming, never-ending quest for status. The right car, house, and connections all testify to the workaholic's sense of worth. Yet he lives in fear of losing it all, and in spite of his "things," he is empty. For others, plastic surgery is their answer for low self-esteem.

Problems such as eating disorders are caused by a wrong self-perception issue. The pencil-thin young woman who has lost too much weight still sees herself as fat and unattractive!

Ex-professional basketball star Wilt Chamberlain states in his book, *A View From Above,* that he had sex with 20,000 women! When a man is insecure about his maleness, he is always looking for someone else to validate him and tell him what he should know for himself.

Wilt joins the ranks of a countless number of athletes, entertainers, politicians, and clergymen who prove you can be famous, have respect, and make millions of dollars, yet see yourself in a totally distorted light.

Think of the professional boxers who have won great success in the ring only to be arrested for brawling or disorderly conduct years later at some seedy bar, or, like Mike Tyson, serve time for rape.

The Bible's answer is:

For as he thinketh in his heart, so is he....

Proverbs 23:7

It cannot be overstated that alcohol, drugs, food, sex, or wrong attitudes are not the problem; they are only *manifestations* of the problem. Simply stated, the problem is not *outside* you; it is *inside* you. When you *believe* something is wrong, you will *do* something wrong.

To achieve wholeness, you must change what you believe — a matter we shall take up as we study cause and effect.

Chapter 4
Cause and Effect

...that they should believe a lie:

That they all might be damned who believed not the truth, but had pleasure in unrighteousness.

2 Thessalonians 2:11,12

Now let us examine elements in our lives that form our beliefs, make us strong, and work for our good — or weaken us and work toward our destruction. We will term this "cause and effect."

Many institutions and counselors, both sacred and secular, spend a great deal of time, money, and energy addressing the causes or symptoms of serious problems.

There is an old saying that goes like this: "When you want to kill something, don't cut off its tail; cut off its head." In other words, *deal with the root of a problem.*

The same principle holds true for people's emotional problems. It is important to understand that for a person to be made whole, the whole person must be dealt with. In fact, it is more important to address *the person* than *the problem,* for what the person *believes* affects the actions and emotions that, in turn, facilitate his problems.

A strong, healthy person can defeat the greatest of problems and overcome great adversity, but a person with a defeated spirit will be overcome by life's smallest tests. He will accept defeat without even putting up a fight, because he *believes* his defeat is inevitable.

19

A defeated person's life is governed by what he *believes* he *can't* do. He says things like, "I *can't* quit smoking." "I *can't* lose weight." "I *can't* save any money." "I *can't* quit drinking."

Such people feel inadequate to raise their children, love their mates, succeed in their job, or simply take charge of their own lives. *Believing* they are defeated before they begin prevents their success. They go through life *believing* that love, happiness, health, success, miracles, and a good marriage come true only for others.

Can't or Won't?

The truth is not that they *can't*, but that they *won't*. They *can* love their spouse and their children. The Bible teaches that love is *a choice*. Otherwise, we would not be *commanded* to love our enemies (Matthew 5:44).

The fact that it takes thought, action, and effort to purchase, light, and smoke a cigarette indicates that all it takes to *quit* smoking is to do nothing! Another example of the power of choice is the fact that it would be nearly impossible for you to *gain* weight if you lowered the amount of calories you ate and increased your exercise routine at the same time.

These simple illustrations are not meant to bring anyone into condemnation. If you are healthy and happy with your weight, that is good. The point is, you will not seek to gain control over the relational, sexual, financial, chemical, or physical areas of your life if you do not *believe* you can.

The Bible's answer is:

I can do all things through Christ which strengtheneth me.

Philippians 4:13

Change What You Believe

Therefore, dealing with the whole person means more than simply making better choices or teaching behavior modification. *It means changing what you believe!*

So alcohol is not your problem. The problem is what you *believe* about alcohol. The deception is that alcohol helps you deal with and fill the voids in your life.

Your extramarital affair manifested something you *believe*. Perhaps the other man or woman made you *feel* important, loved, attractive, and so forth.

Your depression is not caused by circumstances; but, rather, by what you *believe* about those circumstances.

You should say out loud right now:

"I am a person of potential."

"I can do all things through Christ."

"My future is looking brighter."

"I expect good things to happen today."

"God is working all things out for my *good!*"

Only God Can Recreate

Another reason the whole person must be dealt with is, even though what you *believe* causes the problem, its effects are far-reaching.

It is a subtle deception of the devil to make you believe that if you remove the alcohol, the alcoholic is automatically whole. Or, if you remove the pornography, the pervert is normal. Or, if you change the circumstances, the depressed person is cured.

That is why secularists can only sedate, medicate, incarcerate, relocate, and sometimes *rehabilitate*. But only God, through the Holy Spirit, can *recreate!*

If anyone is in Christ, he *is* a new creature. As Weymouth translates Second Corinthians 5:17, "...the old state of things has passed away; a new state of things has come into existence." However, once the spirit of man is *recreated*, his mind must be *renewed*, and his lifestyle *reconstructed*.

Some people are not whole today because they did not deal with the whole person. When persons have been bound by what we call a "life-dominating sin," it is important to understand that although the prayer of faith will save them and deal with the root cause (sin), they must then begin to work on the effects sin once had in their life.

The effects of that sinful former life may be broken relationships, a large debt, or, generally speaking, a life that is out of control. Allowing God to dominate every area of life will bring discipline and a controlled life. *It is discipline that maintains deliverance.*

Far too often we give the Lord only the areas of our life that *we* believe need His attention. Yet most of the time our sin has affected many attitudes, thoughts, feelings, and actions that we have become blind to. Remember, what you *tolerate* will *dominate!*

To achieve total health and wholeness, you must diligently seek God's dominance over your whole being. We will discuss this at length later in this book.

Now I would like to focus our attention on specific areas of concern for our day. Whether you are reading this book for self-help or as a ministry resource to help others, I believe you will be interested in the following areas that affect human behavior.

Chapter 5
Negative Cycles

The chains of a habit are too weak to be felt until they are too strong to be broken.

—Dr. Lester Sumrall

Although he tried to sound strong, the slight crack in the young man's voice betrayed him as I listened to his story.

"Tom," as we will call him, was a successful business-man in his early thirties. Married and the father of three children, Tom had worked hard to better his and his family's life as well as the community where they chose to reside.

Others may have assumed he had everything going for him, but an internal struggle had been hounding Tom for years, robbing him of total freedom and peace. I will never forget the somber, funeral tone of his voice as he spoke of his pain.

It all started, he said, when he was about 10 or 11 years old. "I was playing in my parents' room when I opened their closet door and discovered a two-foot-tall stack of *Playboy* magazines," he recalled. "I rummaged through those magazines, probably more out of curiosity than anything else, taking in all my young eyes and mind would allow."

Tom continued, "Something happened to me that day — I believe a spirit attached itself to me. From that day on, I found my way to my father's closet whenever the opportunity presented itself; and from then on I began to have sexual fantasies about classmates, teachers, and females in general. I saw sexual innuendoes in everything. And that is how it has been for the last 25 years. There have been periodic times of relief, but never freedom. The shame and self-hate it brought has nearly destroyed me."

The good news is that Tom is doing well today. Through strong, earnest prayer; honesty with himself, his wife, and a few friends; accountability; and daily reliance upon the power of the Holy Spirit, Tom has found the power to break this self-debilitating sin. When I spoke to him recently, he told me, "I am freer than I have ever been."

Bound by Lust

The truth is, many people in our society are bound by the awful spirit of lust. Americans spend more than $8 billion a year on pornography. Advertisers use sex to sell everything from toothpaste to tennis shoes.

The result is, our society is facing an epidemic of teenage pregnancies, sexually transmitted diseases (STD) such as gonorrhea, and an alarming rate of AIDS infections and deaths.

The spirit of lust has gained such momentum, countless numbers of people are now bound by such unclean practices as homosexuality, sexual fantasies, wife swapping, masturbation, and countless others; and are scarred by acts of rape, incest, and sexual abuse.

Effects of Sexual Abuse

Statistics show that as many as 38 percent of all women, by the time they reach age 18, have been sexually abused. The figure is between 20 and 30 percent for men, and these numbers are on the rise. And according to a therapist in Washington State, "Sadly, the incidence of sexual abuse is roughly the same in churches."

The seeds sown in a person's childhood through sexual abuse often result in a terrible "harvest" years after the abuse has stopped. It may manifest in depression, nightmares, anxiety attacks, panic attacks, migraine headaches, promiscuity, rebellion, antisocial behavior, violence, drug and alcohol abuse, and even murder or suicide!

These self-destructive patterns are a result of a demonic assault against the victim. Satan uses the trauma of the abuse to gain a stronghold of despair, discouragement, and self-hatred. *These demonic powers must be dealt with and their influence broken before total freedom can come.*

The Horror of Hopelessness

Dr. Stephen B. Seager wrote in *Psycheward* about a patient named Martin, who described what it was like to lose contact with reality.

Dr. Seager quotes the young man as saying, "I know I used to feel things, but now it's like I'm hollow or numb, completely empty. It's as if we are talking across a great divide, like I'm looking at you from the wrong end of binoculars. I know I could physically reach out and touch you, but I can't get a sense of you as a person. Everything is so cold and unreal."

Dr. Seager says, "Martin's voice had a slight monotone drone to it. The words were coming out in correct order, but there was no inflection in them, no up and down, no pauses. It was like they were coming over a teletype."

"Sometimes I think I'm the only person left in the world," Martin told the doctor, "the only person in the entire Universe. It's like I'm floating alone out in a huge, hopeless black void; that no matter how hard I search or how long I float, I will never see another living human being again."

What a powerful and revealing interview! You can almost feel Martin's hopelessness. The sad truth is that many people feel the same way.

Some hear voices that tell them to do destructive things to themselves or others. Others struggle with emotional problems for years, living a presumably normal life until they experience great stress. Then their thoughts may range from suicide to murder, and they may become almost catatonic or violent.

To family and friends who have been unaware of their struggle, their sudden abnormal actions may appear to be out of character and totally out of the blue. In reality, few of these kinds of problems develop suddenly without cause.

The Breaking Point

For example, I recently talked to a teenager who had always been a typical boy: not in too much trouble, and certainly not an angel, either — just your typical, run-of-the-mill 15-year-old.

One evening, to the surprise of his mother, the boy began to run through the house, swearing at the top of his lungs and jumping on furniture. His mother took him to a nearby mental health center, where he told of hearing voices in his room. Then his mother called me.

While praying about the situation on my way to visit this young man, a scripture verse was illuminated to my mind: "...so the curse *causeless* shall not come" (Proverbs 26:2).

There is always a reason. Things don't "just happen." Many factors that contribute to a person's problem may go unnoticed for years; however, if you are able to accurately evaluate his or her life, *you will find the open door through which Satan gained access.*

The Open Door Satan Entered

In this case, I learned that before the young man's mother separated from his natural father, the man was violent and abusive. He would punch his son with his fists. He would also wake his son up in the middle of the night and threaten to stab the boy's mother to death.

Scenes like these were repeated night after night. The father always ended his fits by telling the son that he was going to desecrate a crucifix and a religious statue.

After the boy's mother divorced this ungodly man, it seemed all was well with the boy. However, his seemingly normal life changed when he entered his teenage years. Then the combination of running with the wrong crowd and listening to the wrong music, coupled with his traumatic childhood experiences, made him a prime target for spiritual assault.

It was as if the boy's father had painted a bull's-eye on his back, stripped him of all spiritual armor, and sent him unprotected onto the battlefield of life as easy prey for the enemy of his soul.

After praying for this young man and driving the unclean spirits from him and his home, his future once again looks bright. He's not out of the woods yet, but we haven't given up, either!

How tragic that many people suffer in ignorance, not knowing that Satan will grip their minds and emotions if the opportunity presents itself!

Chapter 6
The Depressed Person

Did you know that psychiatrists treat more cases of depression than any other emotional disturbance? It is estimated that more than 20 million Americans suffer from this problem; and depression occurs twice as often in women than it does in men.

A person who is depressed feels *hopeless* and *helpless*. Many times they also struggle with feelings of *worthlessness*. These negative emotions may eventually affect the person's *physical appearance*. One of the first signs of depression is a general lack of concern for personal appearance.

Those who suffer from depression usually have a general "what's-the-use?" attitude. As a result, they may let their hair go unwashed, uncombed, or uncut, and they may not change their clothes for days. Men may not bother to shave.

Sufferers' facial expressions may become *sad* and *tired* looking. They may want to *sleep* a great deal of the time. They may also feel like *crying*, or they may want to *sit alone* in a darkened room.

Depressed people begin *to worry a lot* about the past, about mistakes both real and imagined, and about the future. They may feel *unloved, unwanted,* and *out of step with reality.* Their powers of *concentration* may become impaired.

A *lack of motivation* caused by wrong thinking and negative feelings is another sign of depression. Those suffering from depression become more and more *reclusive;* they don't want to be around friends or family, and they no longer find pleasure in activities they used to enjoy. They may *lose their sense of humor,* and if they do not receive help, some will become *suicidal.*

The Alarming Rise of Suicides

Suicide is the eighth leading cause of death in the United States. In 1985 alone, some 28,500 Americans took their own lives. And as if that figure isn't startling enough, some estimate that suicide attempts may be 10 times that amount today!

In Toledo, Ohio, where I pastor, the latest reports state that as of 1993, suicide was the third leading cause of death among teenagers.

Ten percent of those who attempt suicide, or make what is termed "suicidal gestures", eventually succeed. Eighty percent of those who commit suicide have warned someone of their intentions. These people must be taken seriously!

The spirit of suicide has gripped them and worked its way into their thought life and emotions. It will destroy them if it is not expelled!

Women attempt suicide five times more often than men. However, twice as many men die from suicide each year. It is thought that men are more successful in their attempts than women because men use more violent means, such as guns, hanging, or crashing their automobile. Women, on the other hand, are more likely to overdose on sleeping pills.

The Theory of Inward Anger

Suicide is the ultimate goal of the spirit that harasses the depressed. Freud said that suicide is inward anger toward another directed at self.

The 19th century sociologist Emile Durkheim related suicide or suicidal attempts to a person's alienation from society. He called it "inverted homicide." In short, his theory is, "...before you kill yourself you must have a repressed desire to kill someone else."

Whether these theories are correct or not, most experts agree that *pent-up anger is the root of nearly all clinical depression.*

Many people who struggle with maintaining wholeness find that their upbringing conditioned them to accept inappropriate responses to life and its pressures as normal. Often unresolved issues and strongholds seek to keep people in bondage, even after they have made a commitment to Christ.

However, God is so completely committed to your freedom, He has sent the Holy Spirit to help you out of your bondage — even if it means temporarily suspending your feelings of self-sufficiency and security until He can work out His wonderful will for your life. Such was the case with Susan, whose story is told in the following chapter.

Chapter 7
Susan's Story

"It's a typical fall Sunday in the Midwest," thought Susan as she drove toward church.

The sun pierced periodically from behind white-gray clouds against a backdrop of brilliant blue sky. Vivid colors shaded the trees which, in a few short weeks, would grudgingly give up their leaves for another season.

And there was a slight nip in the air which brought with it a fragrance of freshness along with the reminder that colder days were ahead.

As Susan drove the last mile to the church, she became aware of the new sense of accomplishment that had filled her life. Perhaps "growth" would be a better word. But whatever the word, her feeling was undeniable: Good things were happening! Her life was on the rise!

For the first time in a long time, "excited" was an adjective her friends now used to describe Susan. She was motivated, anticipating each new day rather than dreading its arrival. It was a good feeling, and Susan wasn't ashamed to say she liked it. Neither was she bashful when questioned by others as to the source of her "new life," as she put it.

Although the words she used varied, her answer was always basically the same. First, she shared that her new life was a result of the forgiveness and acceptance she found in a personal relationship with Jesus Christ. Second, she added that she had found a wonderful church family to worship with. They were "growing and going" together for Jesus, she said happily.

Susan parked her car and hurried into the church. She could hear that the service was just beginning, so she found a seat quickly, not stopping to talk to anyone. She settled herself just as the morning prayer concluded with a rousing "Amen!" from the congregation.

The Joy of Being Part of the Church

Susan felt blessed to be a part of this community of believers. It was nice, she decided, to be where worship and service to God was taken seriously. Each week she was finding new ways to express her praise to God. She was also learning about God's unfailing love and His plan for her life. She had a feeling that everything was going to be all right.

But little did she know her feelings of happiness were soon going to be replaced temporarily by a more sober, unsettling, introspective feeling.

It all started when the pastor, as part of his series on prayer, came to a scripture that began, "Our Father which art in heaven...."

Although Susan did not dare acknowledge it — not even to herself — there was *something* about that phrase that disturbed her. It was not that she didn't believe it, nor that she became angry on hearing it. In fact, it was barely at a conscious level. It was more like a gnawing in the pit of her stomach.

The Power of Repressed Memories

As the pastor continued, Susan took notes and chirped in with a periodic "Amen" of her own. On the outside, Susan looked and acted like all the other parishioners — but on the inside, old, repressed emotions and memories started to rage within her.

The pastor continued. It seemed to Susan that he would never move to another point. Over and over again, he gave illustrations and drove his point home with expert skill that God is our *Father*.

By now, tears were forming in Susan's eyes. She knew she loved God, but she felt as distant from Him as she was from her own human father. By the time music began for the altar call, Susan's insides were shaking.

While the congregation sat with heads bowed, the minister asked all who wanted a closer, more intimate relationship with Father God to stand. Susan stood, not really hearing the pastor's prayer, too preoccupied with her own hurt and wondering if a simple prayer was really going to help heal her lifetime of hurt.

Before the service was over that day, the congregation sang, gave their tithes and offerings, shook hands, and hugged as usual. No one was aware of what was happening to Susan. She smiled and talked as always, seemingly happy.

Being surrounded by others seemed to drown out the raw emotions the message had stirred up. It wasn't until Susan pulled out of the parking lot, alone in her car, that she became aware again of her internal aching. On her way home from church, memories of a lifetime of hurts began to replay in her heart.

An Abnormal Family

Susan was the third and youngest child in what seemed like a perfectly normal family. She remembered how she and her older brothers spent summer days happily playing in the front yard.

But driving home on this autumn day, Susan suddenly wondered if they played outside because they did not want to go into the house, for it was inside the house, among those she loved, that Susan first experienced the pain that haunted her as an adult.

Susan's father was big on public perception and social graces. He wanted his family to look like the perfect little family when they were seen together in public — which was not too often. Several times a month they went to church together. Once a year they attended the annual office Christmas party. Holidays brought a few dreadful reunions with distant relatives and so forth.

Susan's father was "a drinker." That was the way they referred to it in those days. Today we would call him an alcoholic. He was careful never to drink much in public; nor did he ever allow his drinking to affect his work. To most who knew him, he was considered a pretty good guy. It was his family who knew the truth.

Susan unknowingly began to tighten her grip on the steering wheel as she remembered his outbursts of profanity. It seemed to her as a child that his powerful voice shook the entire house. He would rant on and on, shouting words that no one else was allowed to say.

She searched her memory, as she had so many times before, wondering exactly what it was that set him off. And, as always, she had no answer.

Tender Targets of Drunken Wrath

Sometime throughout the course of his rage, Susan's father would begin to single out family members to be targets for his drunken anger. It always began with Susan's mother. "Why mom?" Susan thought, now shaking her head as the old feelings pressed in on her. Her mother was perfect. But no one was good enough for her dad when he was drunk.

Susan remembered the look of fear on her mother's face as her father's rage moved from verbal to physical. He pushed her and threatened her mostly, but Susan never forgot the look of humiliation on her mother's face at the times he doubled up his fists and struck her in front of her children.

Yet it was the children for whom he reserved most of his hostility. He would begin by haranguing them about the evils of the world; how tough life was; and how little they appreciated what they had. He even reminded them of how lucky they were to have *him* as their father. "What a joke!" Susan said out loud in her car.

Her father seemed to view the boys as a group rather than as individuals. He yelled at them together and even beat them together. Whatever one got, both got.

"Special" Treatment for Susan

Susan waited her turn to be singled out. After verbally and physically assaulting her mother and brothers, he would often sit on the stairs or in his recliner. Then he would call for Susan. "Come sit with me," he would say.

At this point, he would begin pouring out a rationale for his actions. Susan remembered the sour smell of alcohol that seemed to engulf him. She remembered his tears as he held her on his lap, explaining why he was so hard on everyone. She also remembered the house being totally silent, with all eyes fixed on them, the others rooted to the spot where his wrath had left them.

"Daddy's Little Girl"

Her father would cry, explain, and apologize. He would tell Susan, "You are the only one who really cares for me. *You are Daddy's little girl.*"

To Susan's young mind, she would rather have been beaten like the rest of the family. It would have been easier to deal with than the emotional trauma of being alienated and separated from the "good guys."

However, no one in the family ever treated her badly because of her father's seeming preferential treatment of her. As a matter of fact, no one ever said *anything* about those early days of abuse, or the tragic years that followed.

By now, Susan had driven into the driveway of her house, but the painful memories had such a hold on her, she was unable to get out of the car.

She remembered the night when "Daddy" rewrote the script. She remembered him putting his hands under her nightie and touching her. She knew it was wrong. She wanted to resist, but no one ever resisted him. Besides, who would rescue her? He would only beat anyone who protested.

Since she did not know what to do, she did nothing. She remembered feeling trapped, humiliated, and frightened as he climbed into her bed with his clothes off. "You are the only one who really loves me," were the words he used as he began what would be several years of incest.

The Legacy of Betrayal

As Susan entered her mid-teens, she found ways to avoid him, and for whatever reason, the incest stopped. But the damage was already done. Susan tried everything she could think of to rid herself of the feelings of guilt, betrayal, and hatred her father's betrayal had left her with.

Many nights she found herself with different boys from school. They didn't care for her; they just wanted to use her. But "Daddy" had taught her well and, more often than not, Susan didn't resist.

Wiping tears from her eyes, Susan finally got out of the car and walked into her house. She plopped down on the couch, and there she realized for the first time how those years had scarred her.

Pieces of the Puzzle Come Together

Fragmented pieces began to fit together: her bouts with depression, her short, failed marriage, and her history of one broken relationship after another.

She was finally able, with the help of the Holy Spirit, to see the whole picture. Her troubled life was not made up of a random series of disconnected events, but, rather, a continuous theme was being played out over and over again!

Susan was not yet fully aware of *why* these feelings were suddenly surfacing now at a time when things seemed to be better for her. She knew she had received Christ's forgiveness, and He was now the most important Person in her life.

An Inspired Prayer

Just before drifting into exhausted sleep, she prayed this powerful little prayer:

"Jesus, I know I'm saved, but I still need some help!"

Have you ever prayed a prayer like that? If not, do it now! You will find the liberating power that comes from confessing before God your dependency on Him! He will start you on a journey to wholeness in Him.

Chapter 8
Striving for Completeness

When striving for completeness in Christ, we can become sidetracked by seeking to attach blame for our problems to someone or something. Although many factors produce cause and effect in our lives, we must remember that how we got here is not so important as how we get out or through our problems that counts!

Mental health professionals, sociologists, and psychiatrists have debated for decades as to what is the greatest contributor to the cause of human behavior.

Some hold to the belief that *environment* is responsible for the way people act. They believe we adapt to our surroundings and carry those experiences with us always.

This theory about environment gives rise to such sayings as, "You can take the boy out of the 'hood,' but you can't take the 'hood' out of the boy."

This is a defeatist theory, and it leads to such excuses as, "I am depraved because I was deprived," "A leopard can't change its spots, you know," and "Once a junkie always a junkie."

Since those who hold to this school of thought seek to blame environment, they absolve the person from any responsibility for his actions.

The person who buys into this belief will generally live in bondage, for if I am not responsible for where I am, I cannot be responsible for where I am going! If everything is the fault of an oppressive society, I will sit passively by while society flounders in efforts to save me.

Others argue that it is not environment that determines behavior; but, rather, *genetics.* They believe that behavior is somehow inherited.

This school of thought believes that just as eye color, skin pigmentation, and height are passed from parent to children, in like manner so are predispositions to certain behavior. They cite as proof the amazing number of children of alcoholics who later follow in the same path as their parents.

Still others would argue that *socialization* plays the biggest role in the development of a child. Those who hold to this theory state that we learn at a young age by watching how parents, peers, and teachers respond to the world.

Then, if we have positive role models, we will do well, but if we are left to ourselves or have poor role models, we will fail miserably.

The Missing Dimension

Although these and other conclusions may have some merit, most of them exclude *the spiritual dimension* of man.

Modern man has all the statistics, signs, and studies necessary to point him to the correct answer. Yet, somehow, like a calculator gone astray, he has all the numbers, but he can't calculate them correctly!

Removed from proper spiritual knowledge and the covering of God's guidance, he is powerless to free himself — or anyone else, for that matter.

In recent years we have seen an effort to redefine good and evil. The philosophy of the day is, "Since we can't be as bad as we seem — you're O.K. and I'm O.K. — what we are doing must not be wrong."

Therefore, we decide we should legalize our evil, or at least take the evil stigma off it. This down-playing of deviance has led to the feeling that we now have the right to question God's eternal laws.

The Proper Conclusion

Our problems, however, are not solvable by government, law enforcement, more money, or better housing. Not until we bring the truth of scripture to the equation can the proper conclusion be realized.

The troubles upon the world today are a result of the curse of sin. As Ezekiel 18:4 states, "...the soul that sinneth, it shall die."

The missing ingredient to the questions modern man has concerning his own behavior is the *spiritual dimension*.

The "Real" World

Although we are unable to see with our eyes the forces which govern the spiritual universe around us, this does not diminish their power or influence.

The unseen world is more *real* than the world we contact through our bodies! Things of a spiritual dimension govern and affect things of the material dimension.

> ...what is seen does not owe its existence to that which is visible.
>
> **Hebrews 11:3** *Weymouth*

For us to properly assess the human condition and correct it, we must look beyond environment, genetics, socialization, and so forth. We must look beyond the natural sphere into the *spiritual realm*, for it is in this dimension that the curse has come, bringing destruction, deviance, and death. Therefore, only in this dimension can the blessing of God overcome the curse, bringing liberty and life.

Evil entities of the spirit world seek to destroy the well-being of God's creation *by gaining access* to their lives. Their primary way of gaining access to mankind is by influencing the thoughts, feelings, and atmosphere that surrounds us.

This, in turn, leads to our sinful actions, iniquity, and perversion.

43

Demonic agents walk through the double doors of iniquity and perversion, bringing with them the curse of sin upon their victims.

We read in James 1:13-15:

[God]...**does not himself tempt anyone. A man is in every case tempted by his own passions — allured and enticed by them. Then passion conceives and gives birth to sin** *(TCNT)*, **and sin when fully matured gives birth to death** *(Wey)*.

God's Protective Natural Laws

The universe owned and created by God has built-in laws which safeguard it from total overthrow by evil forces. These are sometimes referred to as natural laws. *The universe is not designed to facilitate evil!*

Therefore, natural law helps to keep order by intensifying its allowance of hardships upon the perpetrators and peddlers of sin. Such catastrophic events as floods, famines, earthquakes, shortages, and the depletion of ozone and natural resources are a result of the earth's purging itself against the sins of mankind.

All creation is yearning, longing to see the manifestation of the Sons of God.

Romans 8:19,20 *Wey*

Because the universe itself *(NEB)* **shall be delivered from** *(KJV)* **its slavery to death** *(Conybeare)* **into the freedom which belongs to the glory of the children of God** *(Montgomery)*.

Romans 8:21

It is plain to anyone with eyes to see that at the present time all created life groans in a sort of universal travail.

Romans 8:22 *Phillips*

Because God is just, natural law allows evil to come upon mankind as a form of *temporary* recompense for his iniquity.

Evil Cannot Win

There is no possibility for evil to win on the Earth. The Earth is the Lord's. It was created to give man a place to live and to worship God. When its purpose is perverted, a curse comes upon the land. The Earth will self-destruct before it will allow ungodly men to possess it!

According to the Genesis account (Genesis 2:7), man is made from the same substance that makes up the Earth: dust! Just as the Earth is the Lord's, the body also belongs to the Lord. When His purposes for our body are perverted, the body gives way to hardships of every description.

When dealing with something like AIDS, we must understand it is not that God has put this on people; but rather, it is the law of recompense in operation:

> **For we see the divine retribution revealed from heaven falling upon all the godless wickedness of men....**
>
> **Romans 1:18 *NEB***

> **For this cause God gave them up unto vile affections. Even the women among them perverted the natural use of their bodies to unnatural.**
>
> **Romans 1:26 *TCNT***

> **...But the men also, in the same way, neglecting sexual intercourse with women, have burned fiercely in their lust for one another *(Wey)*. Men committing shameless acts with men *(Revised Standard Version)*, and receiving in themselves that recompense of their error which was due *(American Standard Version)*.**
>
> **Romans 1:27**

This sheds light on the question modern unbelieving man asks about why those who have not participated in the sin can also be affected by it. For example, there are children and adults who have AIDS, but never committed homosexual acts. They are usually either family members of AIDS patients, or persons who received transfusions of tainted blood.

Why the Innocent Suffer

Similarly, thousands of babies are born in this country already addicted to crack. Other children are abused and suffer through no fault of their own. Why? *The root cause is sin, iniquity, and perversion in mankind.*

The law of recompense allows temporary intense hardships to occur. Its purpose is for men to see the error of their ways and repent. If, under the law of recompense, a man rejects God, it will lead to judgment. The law of recompense is only *temporary* payment, but the judgment of God is *eternal.*

Repentance is the door Jesus walks through to bring restoration! He states in the Book of Revelation:

Behold, I stand at the door, and knock: if any man hear my voice, and open the door, I will come in to him, and will sup with him, and he with me.

Revelation 3:20

Chapter 9
Breaking the Cycle

Therefore if any man be in Christ, he is a new creature: old things are passed away; behold, all things are become new.

2 Corinthians 5:17

When true repentance is experienced, the Holy Spirit works on behalf of the saved person to bring his *condition* in line with his new *position.*

In the mind of God, all things we need pertaining to salvation and a godly life are *already ours!* When the Lord Jesus Christ, after his death, burial, and resurrection, sat down at the right hand of the Father, all was *finished.* God has already forgiven the whole world!

Forgiveness has already been credited to your account. However, for you to *really experience it,* you must make a "withdrawal" by faith.

The Poor Rich Woman

I am reminded of a story about a woman who worked for many years as a faithful housekeeper for a wealthy man. She had come from an impoverished family and had little education. In fact, she couldn't read. Therefore, she considered herself very fortunate when at a young age she was asked to work for the tycoon.

Finally it became evident that the rich man's health was failing him. He had no family, and no friends came to visit him. As the story goes, late one night the man sketched out his will, leaving his entire fortune to the housekeeper who had been so kind to him all those years.

After finishing the will, he signed it and put it in a glass picture frame which included a small portrait of himself in the corner. He then wrapped the frame, intending to present it to the housekeeper in the morning. The rich man never saw the light of day, however, for he died in the night.

When the housekeeper lay dying some years later, her surroundings greatly contrasted with those of her former employer.

She lay in a rickety old bed, but she was surrounded by friends and family. Her bedclothes were tattered and worn, and her little shack showed the signs of neglect and poverty.

As the end neared, conversation turned to the kind tycoon for whom she had worked. With shaking hands, she reached into the night stand beside her bed and pulled out the old picture frame, its bow still intact.

An Old Piece of Paper

With a weak laugh she said, "You know, the only thing that man ever gave me was this piece of paper and his picture." One of her sons took it from her and silently read the document the frame had held for so many years.

Tears fell from his eyes as he realized in amazement that his mother had lived her life in terrible poverty when, in fact, she was a wealthy woman, for the tycoon had left his faithful servant all his riches!

So it is with the things pertaining to salvation. It is possible for you to possess something "technically," "theologically," or "positionally," but not have it *in reality*.

Breaking Cycles of Sin

This needs to be stressed, because so many well-meaning, praying people are still fighting the negative effects of this cycle of sin that has existed sometimes for generations in their families.

Although it is true that we are free, healed, delivered, and blessed as a result of salvation, often there is a battle between what is ours *legally* and what we are actually possessing and experiencing at the present time.

To bring the reality of salvation into existence in your life, you must do three things: (1) *seek*, (2) *surrender*, and (3) *study*.

Seek

But seek ye first the kingdom of God, and his righteousness; and all these things shall be added unto you.

Matthew 6:33

You must have a desire to have God's kingdom established in your heart. Your heart must *long* to have Jesus make His will known to you. It is out of your desires that priorities are set. *Pursuit is the proof of desire!*

You must seek the Lord if you are to create the right desires in your heart. This will give way to proper priorities and pursuits in your life. Many people wait until they have a desire to seek God before they pray, but that is not the way spiritual life works.

The more you seek God, the greater your desire and capacity for Him will be. The less you seek Him, the greater the possibility that wrong desires, priorities, and pursuits will dominate your life.

So seek the Lord, not out of guilt or ritual, but because it is in Him that we really live and have our being! I believe that a fresh anointing to seek the Lord is birthing in you right now. Yield to it! Grow in it in Jesus' Name.

Surrender

Saying, Father, if thou be willing, remove this cup from me: nevertheless not my will, but thine be done.

Luke 22:42

When you seek the Lord, one of the results of being in His presence is insight — insight into circumstances, self, and His eternal purposes.

When, through the Holy Spirit, you begin to gain insight, you must have a strong commitment to follow through with what you have been shown.

For example, you may gain insight into why, in certain environments, you react in particular ways. The Spirit may be instructing you to avoid certain settings or controlling persons.

Then again, His direction may be for you to change your attitude, conversation, or so forth. Whatever it may be, you must be totally committed to surrender to His guidance.

Self-awareness can be painful. Most people never get to the place of total freedom and wholeness in Christ because they are not willing to work through the remolding of their life.

Study

All scripture is given by inspiration of God, and is profitable for doctrine, for reproof, for correction, for instruction in righteousness:

That the man of God may be perfect, thoroughly furnished unto all good works.

2 Timothy 3:16,17

You must also develop a proper relationship with the Word of God. You must begin to see it as your *daily* source for spiritual strength. The Bible is not a book of magic spells and formulas; it is a spiritual book containing truth and godly principles!

When you develop a proper relationship with the Word, your inner man becomes strong. The Holy Spirit highlights and illuminates the divine principles of scripture when you seek God's kingdom, and a positive pattern of power begins to emerge in your life.

First, as you seek God's kingdom, your desire and capacity for Him increases.

Second, this desire and closeness makes you want to surrender your will to His. It allows the King to set up His rule in your heart.

Third, as you study, you find that the principles and truth of His kingdom empower you to change.

Renewing the Mind

The information you receive determines what you believe. The mind that is overly influenced by negative information is not free to live a positive life.

For as he thinketh in his heart, so is he....

Proverbs 23:7

Stress, frustration, and internal conflict result when a person strives to live a life that his internal beliefs won't allow him to.

Once salvation has occurred, a process must begin: You must begin to think in a way you have never thought before.

A large factor in the bondage of addictions (chemical, sexual, food, or material) is aided by a network of beliefs that only insure continued dependency!

Often people develop great rationales, philosophies, and even religious doctrines to excuse their bondage. However, when Jesus comes into a person's life, He aggressively attacks the strongholds that hold the person under their tyranny.

Therefore, *you must change what you think* if you hope to be the whole person Christ desires you to be.

And do not follow the customs of the present age, but be transformed by the entire renewal of your minds.

Romans 12:2 *Wey*

Lives Built on Sand

Sometimes it is difficult for us to deal with the strongholds that have developed in our minds. To bring them down means we must first admit the painful reality that we have lived limited lives built on sand.

Now Jesus comes to bring freedom to us, and the step we must now take is the policing of our thoughts — the systems by which we process information and the value judgments we give to the influences of our mind.

that you put off, concerning your former conduct, the old man which grows corrupt according to the deceitful lusts,

and be renewed in the spirit of your mind.

Ephesians 4:22,23 *NKJV*

As this scripture continues, notice you are only able to properly develop new thoughts as the old ones are put off.

and that you put on the new man which was created according to God, in righteousness and true holiness.

Ephesians 4:24 *NKJV*

If a person who is finding freedom and/or deliverance does not first allow the old to be put off and new thoughts to be put on, old strongholds of fear, poverty, domination, control, anger, pride, and low self-esteem may overtake him again.

It is easy to think and dwell on the negative. It is too easy to walk in the humanistic philosophies of ungodly people around us. It is too easy to reflect over all the failures of our life, wishing some things hadn't happened, and to dream of what could have been. It's just too easy to be defeated — and that's why so many people are!

A New Day Dawns for You

A new day is beginning for you. I am excited for you! God is going to show you a new way of thinking; a new way of believing; a new way of living. *He is TRANSFORMING you!*

This word "transform" in its Greek form is *metamorpho*. We derive the word "metamorphosis" from this root. The most common example is the process of change a caterpillar goes through.

After entering its cocoon, there is a season of change — a transformation, a metamorphosis. When that season is completed, what emerges from the cocoon is so drastically different from what entered it that a new name must be given to it! It is no longer an ugly caterpillar; it is a beautiful *butterfly!*

You are in your season of change, transformation, and metamorphosis; and when you emerge, you won't think of yourself as a *recovering* alcoholic, a *survivor* of incest, or a *former* drug addict.

Why? Because you will emerge so drastically different from your position of bondage until the old labels and adjectives used to describe you will become obsolete. You really have become *a new creature in Christ Jesus!*

Chapter 10
Free at Last!

God has placed in the deepest part of every man the desire to be free. History tells us when a people are enslaved, they will overcome unbelievable obstacles and do extraordinary things to achieve independence.

We have such a great heart for deliverance and freedom, we immortalize famous people and the events surrounding them. The parting of the Red Sea, the Boston Tea Party, the Montgomery bus boycott, Ghandi's hunger strikes, and Schindler's list — all evoke the powerful passion of the human spirit's ability to triumph over oppression. Yet man is limited dimensionally in the extent of his delivering power.

Jesus, however, is not. He has stepped upon the stage of human history to free all of mankind from its diverse bondages.

Jesus Set the Captives Free

Jesus freed the man of Gadarene from demon power.

He liberated the woman taken in adultery from her self-righteous accusers.

He mobilized the paralyzed and made the withered hand work again.

He put focus in the dim eye of the blind and flooded with sound the silent world of the deaf.

He loosed the tongue of the mute and silenced the threatening storm.

He fed the hungry multitudes and called Lazarus out of his four-day grave.

He lived, moved, and taught; in all that He did demonstrating to us God's supreme will that we live free from bondage and hindrance.

Then in one epic scene, like the star of a universal play, the Messenger of freedom hung suspended between heaven and Earth.

The voice of a criminal on one side of him jeered, "If you are the Son of God, save yourself and us" (Luke 23:39).

Freedom for All

Yet Jesus the miracle man stayed true to His Father's master plan for liberation. Through His sacrifice on the cross and His subsequent burial and resurrection, He purchased freedom for all who would call upon His name.

Now He Himself, freed from the physical limitations of a human body, enforces His authority over bondage by the Holy Spirit in and through His modern-day disciples, who we are. Call upon His name and know the power of His great salvation — a saving for the whole man: spirit, soul, and body; a saving for all time: past, present and future.

I am so glad I can say...

My spirit has been saved

My soul is in the process of being saved

My body will be saved in the Resurrection.

I can say...

I have been delivered from the penalty of sin.

I am being delivered from the power of sin.

I shall be delivered from the presence of sin.

Now let the compassion of God flow through you for the suffering, the bound, and the oppressed. Go in His love, in His strength, and in His name.

And these signs shall follow them that believe; In my name shall they cast out devils; they shall speak with new tongues;

They shall take up serpents, and if they drink any deadly thing, it shall not hurt them; they shall lay hands on the sick, and they shall recover.

Mark 16:17,18

For a complete list of books and tapes by Michael S. Pitts,
or to contact him for speaking engagements,
please write or call:

Pitts Evangelistic Association
P.O. Box 351690
Toledo, OH 43635
(419) 865-5453